CROCK POT COOKBOOK FOR WOMEN OVER 70

1000+ Easy Crock Pot Recipes for Women Over 70

Elsie Dill

Copyright

© 2024 by Elsie Dill

All rights reserved. No part of this publication may be reproduced, distributed, or transmitted in any form or by any means, including photocopying, recording, or other electronic or mechanical methods, without the prior written permission of the publisher, except in the case of brief quotations embodied in critical reviews and certain other non-commercial uses permitted by copyright law.

Disclaimer

The information in this book is provided for general informational purposes only. The author makes no warranties about the accuracy, completeness, or suitability of the content. Any reliance you place on the information is at your own risk. This book is not a substitute for professional advice, and the author disclaims any liability for any loss or damage incurred. The inclusion of third-party links does not imply endorsement. This is a work of fiction/non-fiction (specify), and any resemblance to real persons or events is coincidental. Unauthorized reproduction or distribution is prohibited. The case studies and examples in this book are fictional and for illustrative purposes only. Any resemblance to real events or persons, living or dead, is coincidental. The author retains all rights.

About the Author

Elsie Dill, a seasoned voice in the realm of adolescent empowerment. At the age of 43, Elsie's commitment to understanding the intricate challenges faced by teenagers has become a driving force behind her work.

A proud American, Elsie hails from a diverse background, and her experiences have fuelled her passion for fostering resilience and strength in young minds. As a white author, she recognizes the importance of embracing diversity and inclusivity in every facet of a teenager's journey.

With a background in psychology and personal development, Elsie combines her professional expertise with a genuine understanding of the nuanced struggles that come with adolescence. Her dedication to empowering teens is evident in the thoughtful guidance and practical advice found within the pages of this book. Her commitment to making a positive impact on the lives of young individuals extends beyond the written word.

Elsie Dill invites readers to embark on a transformative journey through where her insights and encouragement aim to inspire and guide teenagers toward embracing their strength and navigating the complexities of adolescence with resilience.

Table of Contents

CHAPTER ONE: GETTING STARTED WITH YOUR CROCK POT 15

    How to Use This Cookbook 15

    Benefits of Crock Pot Cooking 16

    Key Tips for Success 18

    Essentials for Your Crock Pot Pantry 20

CHAPTER TWO: HEARTY SOUPS & STEWS 25

    Classic Chicken Noodle Soup 25

    Beef and Barley Stew 27

    Creamy Potato Leek Soup 28

    Vegetable Lentil Soup 30

    Savory Split Pea Soup 31

    Chicken and Wild Rice Soup 33

    Hearty Mushroom and Barley Stew 34

    Minestrone with Fresh Vegetables 35

CHAPTER THREE: SAVORY ROASTS & MEATS 37

    Classic Pot Roast with Root Vegetables ... 37

    Tender Pork Loin with Apples 39

    Herb-Infused Lamb Roast 40

    Simple BBQ Pulled Pork 41

    Honey Garlic Chicken Thighs 42

    Braised Short Ribs 44

Lemon Herb Turkey Breast 45

Italian Meatballs in Tomato Sauce 46

CHAPTER FOUR: LIGHT AND FRESH DISHES 49

Lemon Garlic Chicken Breast 49

Vegetable Medley with Fresh Herbs 51

Asian-Inspired Sweet and Sour Chicken 52

Mediterranean Ratatouille 53

Stuffed Bell Peppers 55

Zucchini Lasagna 56

Lemon Dill Salmon 57

Quinoa and Black Bean Casserole 59

CHAPTER FIVE: SIDES & VEGETABLES 61

Garlic Mashed Potatoes 61

Creamed Spinach 62

Green Bean Casserole 63

Herb Buttered Carrots 65

Cheesy Cauliflower Bake 66

Maple-Glazed Sweet Potatoes 67

Brown Rice Pilaf with Veggies 68

Roasted Brussels Sprouts with Bacon 69

CHAPTER SIX: SWEET TREATS & DESSERTS 71

Apple Cinnamon Crisp 71

Vanilla Rice Pudding 73

Chocolate Lava Cake 74

Berry Cobbler 76

Pumpkin Spice Bread Pudding 77

Caramelized Pears 78

Banana Bread 80

Classic Bread Pudding 81

CHAPTER SEVEN: HEALTHY OPTIONS FOR SPECIAL DIETS 83

Low-Sodium Beef Stew 83

Heart-Healthy Chicken and Vegetables 85

Gluten-Free Chili 86

Low-Carb Chicken Alfredo 88

Dairy-Free Vegetable Soup 89

Mediterranean-Inspired Chickpea Stew 90

High-Protein Bean Soup 92

Fiber-Rich Lentil Soup 93

CHAPTER EIGHT: TIME-SAVING TIPS AND MEAL PREP 95

Make-Ahead Meals for Busy Days 95

Freezer-Friendly Crock Pot Recipes 97

Batch Cooking Tips 99

Maximizing Flavor in Your Dishes 101

Tips for Cooking Different Types of Meat 102

  Cleanup and Storage Hacks.................................104
CHAPTER NINE: CONCLUSION 105
  Embracing the Convenience of Slow Cooking 106
  Encouragement to Explore and Experiment 106
  Final Thoughts and Closing Remarks 107

50 Quick & Healthy Crock Pot Recipes for Ageless Wellness!

Welcome to Your Bonus Recipe Collection!
Discover 50 specially selected recipes crafted to bring you wholesome flavors, essential nutrients, and the ease of Crock Pot cooking—all designed to support vibrant health and effortless meal prep.

Section 1: Energizing Breakfasts
Start your day right with nourishing breakfast ideas that warm your body and fuel your morning.

- Overnight Oatmeal with Berries
- Spiced Apple Quinoa
- Protein-Packed Veggie Scramble

Section 2: Hearty Soups & Stews
Fill up on comforting soups and stews packed with vitamins, fiber, and flavor.

- Golden Turmeric Lentil Soup
- Vegetable-Loaded Chicken Stew
- Immune-Boosting Mushroom Broth

Section 3: Lean Proteins & Veggie Dishes
Light and balanced meals perfect for lunch or dinner, keeping your energy up and your health in focus.

- Lemon Herb Chicken with Asparagus
- Southwest Black Bean & Quinoa Bowl
- Stuffed Bell Peppers with Brown Rice

Section 4: Low-Carb & Heart-Healthy Options
Recipes designed for those watching carbs or prioritizing heart health without sacrificing flavor.

- Garlic Butter Salmon with Spinach
- Cauliflower Mashed "Potatoes"
- Heart-Healthy Beef Stew

Section 5: Guilt-Free Desserts
Indulge in sweet treats that satisfy cravings while supporting your wellness goals.

- Berry Compote with Greek Yogurt
- Vanilla Chia Seed Pudding
- Warm Cinnamon Apples

Cooking Tips for Ageless Wellness
Enhance these recipes with simple tips for maximum flavor and nutrition:

- Use fresh herbs and spices to boost taste without extra salt.
- Choose lean cuts and trim any excess fat to keep meals heart-friendly.
- Add colorful veggies to meals to ensure a range of nutrients.

Enjoy every recipe and embrace the ease of wellness cooking with your Crock Pot!

CHAPTER ONE: GETTING STARTED WITH YOUR CROCK POT

How to Use This Cookbook

This cookbook is crafted with you in mind—simple, straightforward recipes that fit seamlessly into your daily routine. Organized by types of dishes, from savory soups and stews to hearty main courses and delightful desserts, you'll find a variety of options to suit any craving or occasion.

Each recipe has clear, easy-to-follow instructions. This structure allows you to quickly scan through ingredient lists and directions, so there's no need to decipher complex cooking techniques or measurements. You'll see basic info at the top of each recipe:

- Prep Time: How long it'll take to get ingredients ready before cooking.
- Cook Time: The time your Crock Pot needs to work its magic.

- Serving Size: Helps with planning, especially if you're cooking for family or making extra for the week.

If you're looking for specific types of meals, the table of contents is organized for quick navigation. Want a light vegetable stew? Go to the soups section. Looking for a classic roast? Flip to the meats chapter. Need something sweet to finish off the meal? Head to desserts. This layout makes it easy to jump straight to the recipes that fit your needs.

Benefits of Crock Pot Cooking

The Crock Pot brings a world of convenience, especially when preparing meals for busy days or for times when you don't want to spend hours standing over the stove. Here's why Crock Pot cooking is especially valuable:

1. Hands-Off Cooking: One of the greatest advantages of the Crock Pot is that it's truly "set and forget." Unlike stovetop or oven cooking, there's no need to stir, flip, or keep a close eye on things. Simply set the temperature and timer, then go about your day while your meal slowly cooks to perfection.

2. Enhanced Flavors: The slow-cooking process lets flavors develop more deeply. As ingredients cook at low temperatures over several hours, they blend harmoniously, enhancing the richness of dishes without needing a lot of added seasonings or complex preparation steps.

3. Tenderizes Tough Cuts of Meat: The Crock Pot is excellent for cooking tougher cuts of meat, like chuck roast or pork shoulder, which become tender and juicy as they simmer. This allows you to enjoy flavorful meats without the higher cost of more tender cuts.

4. Nutrient Retention: Slow cooking keeps the lid on, which helps retain moisture and nutrients, especially for vegetables. Because it uses lower heat, more vitamins and minerals stay intact compared to high-temperature cooking methods.

5. Saves Time and Energy: Besides reducing active cooking time, Crock Pots are energy-efficient compared to traditional ovens or stovetops. They use less electricity, making them an economical choice.

6. Perfect for Batch Cooking: Whether you're cooking for a group or prefer meal-prepping for the week, the Crock Pot makes it easy to double or even triple recipes. Many dishes store well, so you can enjoy leftovers or freeze portions for later.

Key Tips for Success

Making the most out of your Crock Pot requires a few strategies to ensure meals turn out as delicious as possible. These tips will help you avoid common slow-cooking pitfalls, giving you confidence with every dish.

1. Layer Ingredients Strategically
   - Placing ingredients in the right order can affect how they cook. Dense or starchy vegetables (like potatoes, carrots, or root vegetables) should go at the bottom because they need more time and heat to cook thoroughly. Meats and other ingredients that cook faster can be layered on top.

2. Prep Ingredients Ahead of Time
   - Consider chopping vegetables, trimming meats, or measuring out spices the night before. In the morning, you can simply transfer everything to the

Crock Pot, minimizing morning prep time. This approach is especially useful if you have busy days.

3. Minimize Opening the Lid
   - Each time you lift the lid, you release steam and reduce the temperature, which can add to your cooking time. Try to resist the temptation to check in too often, especially in the first few hours.

4. Use Less Liquid than Usual
   - Because Crock Pots don't allow much evaporation, meals tend to retain moisture. Use less liquid than you might normally use on the stove. For example, if you're making a soup, a little broth goes a long way since vegetables release their own juices as they cook.

5. Trim Fats from Meats
   - Fat doesn't render the same way in a slow cooker as it does in an oven, so too much fat can result in a greasy texture. Trim excess fat from meats before adding them to your Crock Pot, especially for dishes like roasts and stews.

6. Choose the Right Setting
   - Most Crock Pots have two primary settings: low and high. While both will get the job done, the low setting (generally cooking for 6–8 hours) is ideal for

tougher meats and recipes that benefit from longer cooking times. High (usually around 3–4 hours) works well when you need food ready sooner or when cooking tender vegetables and grains.

7. Finish with Fresh Herbs or Acids for Flavor
   - Adding a splash of vinegar, lemon juice, or fresh herbs at the end brightens flavors, balancing the richness of slow-cooked dishes. A hint of fresh ingredients can add a new dimension and elevate the final dish.

Essentials for Your Crock Pot Pantry

Having a well-stocked pantry with Crock Pot-friendly ingredients ensures you're always prepared to whip up a meal without last-minute trips to the store. Here's a list of staples that will serve you well for a variety of recipes in this book:

1. Canned Tomatoes and Sauces
   - Tomatoes, whether diced, pureed, or in sauce form, are an essential base for stews, soups, and roasts. They add natural sweetness and acidity, which balances out the flavors of savory dishes.

2. Broths and Stocks
   - Low-sodium chicken, beef, and vegetable broths provide depth without overpowering dishes. Broths help keep dishes moist, but remember to add less in a Crock Pot than you would on the stove.

3. Herbs and Spices
   - Dried herbs like thyme, rosemary, basil, and oregano, along with spices such as cumin, paprika, and bay leaves, will add layers of flavor. Having a few spices on hand means you can easily vary flavors without needing fresh herbs.

4. Beans and Lentils
   - Canned beans, such as black beans, chickpeas, and kidney beans, are nutritious and filling. Lentils are perfect for adding texture to soups and stews and work well in vegetarian dishes for added protein.

5. Rice and Grains
   - Brown rice, quinoa, and barley can be used to create hearty meals in the Crock Pot. Keep in mind that grains absorb a lot of liquid, so adjust recipes accordingly.

6. Vinegars and Condiments
   - Balsamic vinegar, soy sauce, Worcestershire sauce, and Dijon mustard add complexity to dishes.

These small but impactful ingredients can elevate the flavors of meats, stews, and marinades.

7. Frozen Vegetables
   - Frozen peas, corn, spinach, and mixed vegetables are time-savers. They're great for adding nutrition to any dish and are ready to go when you need them.

8. Basic Fresh Vegetables
   - Onions, carrots, celery, garlic, and potatoes form the "holy trinity" of many recipes, adding a base of flavor and texture. Root vegetables hold up well in the slow cooker and add richness to soups and stews.

9. Cooking Oils and Fats
   - Olive oil, vegetable oil, and butter are essentials for sautéing or browning meat before adding to the Crock Pot. This step, while optional, can help enhance flavors.

10. Sweeteners
    - Brown sugar, honey, or maple syrup adds subtle sweetness, which can balance acidic flavors, especially in barbecue sauces and tomato-based dishes.

Having these items on hand means you can create a wide range of dishes without constantly shopping for new ingredients. Adjust your pantry to suit your tastes, and feel free to experiment as you become more comfortable with your Crock Pot.

These detailed insights aim to give you a smooth start on your Crock Pot journey, making cooking both enjoyable and practical. Embrace the ease of slow cooking with these handy tips, and you'll soon find yourself creating comforting, flavorful meals that bring joy to the table every day.

CHAPTER TWO: HEARTY SOUPS & STEWS

This chapter introduces a variety of wholesome, nourishing soups and stews that are perfect for every season. With the Crock Pot, these comforting dishes are as easy as setting the ingredients and letting time do the work, bringing out rich flavors without hours of active cooking. These soups and stews are ideal for cozy nights or when you want a satisfying meal with minimal fuss. Each recipe below is crafted to give you delicious results that you'll want to make again and again.

Classic Chicken Noodle Soup

Prep Time: 15 minutes
Cook Time: 6-8 hours on Low or 3-4 hours on High
Servings: 6

Nothing beats a classic chicken noodle soup, especially when you want something warm and nourishing. This recipe combines tender chicken, hearty noodles, and a blend of vegetables, making it perfect for a comforting lunch or light dinner.

Ingredients:

- 2 boneless, skinless chicken breasts
- 4 cups low-sodium chicken broth
- 2 cups water
- 2 carrots, sliced
- 2 celery stalks, sliced
- 1 small onion, chopped
- 2 cloves garlic, minced
- 1 teaspoon dried thyme
- 1 teaspoon salt
- 1/2 teaspoon black pepper
- 1 cup egg noodles
- Fresh parsley, for garnish

Instructions:

1. Place chicken breasts in the Crock Pot along with the broth, water, carrots, celery, onion, garlic, thyme, salt, and pepper.
2. Cover and cook on Low for 6-8 hours, or on High for 3-4 hours.
3. Remove chicken, shred with forks, and return to the pot.
4. Add egg noodles and cook for another 20-30 minutes, until noodles are tender.
5. Serve hot, garnished with fresh parsley.

Beef and Barley Stew

Prep Time: 20 minutes
Cook Time: 7-8 hours on Low or 4-5 hours on High
Servings: 6

This hearty beef and barley stew is full of flavor and texture. The barley adds a delightful chewiness that complements the tender beef and vegetables, creating a satisfying meal in a bowl.

Ingredients:

- 1 pound beef stew meat, cubed
- 5 cups beef broth
- 1 cup barley
- 3 carrots, sliced
- 2 celery stalks, chopped
- 1 medium onion, chopped
- 2 cloves garlic, minced
- 1 bay leaf
- 1 teaspoon dried thyme
- Salt and pepper to taste

Instructions:

1. Add all ingredients to the Crock Pot, layering the beef at the bottom for even cooking.
2. Stir gently to combine, cover, and cook on Low for 7-8 hours or on High for 4-5 hours.
3. Before serving, remove bay leaf, season with additional salt and pepper if needed, and stir well.
4. Ladle into bowls and enjoy the rich, earthy flavors.

Creamy Potato Leek Soup

Prep Time: 15 minutes
Cook Time: 6-7 hours on Low or 3-4 hours on High
Servings: 6

Creamy, comforting, and perfect for chilly days, this potato leek soup is easy to make and loaded with flavor. The leeks bring a mild, sweet onion flavor that complements the creaminess of the potatoes.

Ingredients:

- 4 large potatoes, peeled and diced
- 2 leeks, thinly sliced (white and light green parts only)
- 4 cups chicken or vegetable broth
- 1 cup milk or cream (for added richness)
- 2 cloves garlic, minced
- Salt and pepper to taste
- Chopped chives, for garnish

Instructions:

1. Place potatoes, leeks, broth, and garlic in the Crock Pot.
2. Cover and cook on Low for 6-7 hours or on High for 3-4 hours, until potatoes are tender.
3. Use an immersion blender to puree the soup until smooth (or transfer in batches to a blender).
4. Stir in milk or cream, season with salt and pepper, and heat for 10 more minutes.
5. Serve hot, garnished with chives.

Vegetable Lentil Soup

Prep Time: 15 minutes
Cook Time: 6-8 hours on Low or 3-4 hours on High
Servings: 6

Packed with fiber and protein, this vegetable lentil soup is a great option for a filling, vegetarian-friendly meal. The lentils cook to a tender perfection, blending beautifully with seasonal vegetables.

Ingredients:

- 1 cup dried green or brown lentils, rinsed
- 4 cups vegetable broth
- 1 can (14.5 oz) diced tomatoes, undrained
- 2 carrots, chopped
- 2 celery stalks, chopped
- 1 small zucchini, diced
- 1 onion, chopped
- 2 cloves garlic, minced
- 1 teaspoon dried basil
- Salt and pepper to taste

> **Instructions:**

1. Combine all ingredients in the Crock Pot and stir well.
2. Cover and cook on Low for 6-8 hours or on High for 3-4 hours, until lentils are tender.
3. Taste and adjust seasonings if needed.
4. Ladle into bowls and serve, perhaps with a sprinkle of grated cheese or fresh herbs.

Savory Split Pea Soup

Prep Time: 10 minutes
Cook Time: 6-8 hours on Low or 3-4 hours on High
Servings: 6

Split pea soup is a classic comfort food, especially with the addition of smoky ham or bacon. This version is easy, hearty, and ideal for cold days when you want something warm and filling.

Ingredients:

- 1 1/2 cups split peas, rinsed
- 4 cups chicken or vegetable broth
- 1 cup water
- 1 onion, chopped
- 2 carrots, chopped
- 2 celery stalks, chopped
- 1 smoked ham hock or 4 slices bacon, diced
- Salt and pepper to taste

Instructions:

1. Add all ingredients to the Crock Pot, making sure split peas are at the bottom for even cooking.
2. Cover and cook on Low for 6-8 hours or on High for 3-4 hours, until peas are soft and soup is thickened.
3. If using a ham hock, remove, shred meat, and return it to the pot.
4. Adjust seasonings and serve hot.

Chicken and Wild Rice Soup

Prep Time: 20 minutes
Cook Time: 6-8 hours on Low or 3-4 hours on High
Servings: 6

This creamy chicken and wild rice soup is deliciously satisfying. The nutty flavor of wild rice pairs beautifully with tender chicken and savory vegetables.

Ingredients:

- 2 boneless, skinless chicken breasts
- 4 cups chicken broth
- 1 cup wild rice, rinsed
- 2 carrots, diced
- 2 celery stalks, diced
- 1 onion, chopped
- 1 teaspoon dried thyme
- 1/2 cup cream (optional)
- Salt and pepper to taste

Instructions:

1. Add all ingredients except the cream to the Crock Pot, layering chicken on top.
2. Cover and cook on Low for 6-8 hours or on High for 3-4 hours, until chicken and rice are tender.
3. Remove chicken, shred, and return to the pot. Stir in cream if desired.
4. Serve warm, and enjoy the creamy, comforting flavors.

Hearty Mushroom and Barley Stew

Prep Time: 15 minutes
Cook Time: 6-8 hours on Low or 3-4 hours on High
Servings: 6

This vegetarian mushroom and barley stew is earthy, filling, and full of fiber and nutrients. The mushrooms add a meaty texture, making it a satisfying meal without the meat.

Ingredients:

- 1-pound mushrooms, sliced
- 4 cups vegetable broth
- 1 cup pearl barley
- 2 carrots, sliced
- 1 onion, chopped
- 2 cloves garlic, minced
- 1 bay leaf
- Salt and pepper to taste

Instructions:

1. Place all ingredients in the Crock Pot and stir gently.
2. Cover and cook on Low for 6-8 hours or on High for 3-4 hours, until barley and vegetables are tender.
3. Remove Bay leaf, taste, and adjust seasonings as needed.
4. Ladle into bowls, garnish if desired, and serve.

Minestrone with Fresh Vegetables

Prep Time: 20 minutes
Cook Time: 6-8 hours on Low or 3-4 hours on High
Servings: 6

This classic Italian soup is loaded with vegetables and pasta, making it a hearty and healthy choice. Feel free to use any seasonal veggies for variety.

Ingredients:

- 1 can (14.5 oz) diced tomatoes
- 4 cups vegetable broth
- 1 zucchini, diced

CHAPTER THREE: SAVORY ROASTS & MEATS

For those who crave the hearty, comforting flavors of slow-cooked meats, this chapter is filled with recipes that bring out the best in roasts, poultry, and meat dishes. These recipes are crafted to maximize tenderness and flavor, allowing you to enjoy mouthwatering meals with minimal effort. Each recipe is straightforward, with easy-to-find ingredients and clear instructions for delicious results.

Classic Pot Roast with Root Vegetables

There's nothing quite like a classic pot roast with root vegetables, simmered until tender and full of flavor. This recipe combines the rich, savory taste of beef with the earthy sweetness of carrots, potatoes, and onions.

Ingredients:

- 3 lb beef chuck roast
- 4 carrots, peeled and chopped
- 4 potatoes, quartered
- 1 large onion, sliced
- 3 garlic cloves, minced
- 1 cup beef broth
- 1 tbsp Worcestershire sauce
- 1 tsp thyme
- 1 tsp rosemary
- Salt and pepper to taste

Instructions:

1. Season the roast with salt and pepper.
2. Place the chopped carrots, potatoes, onion, and garlic at the bottom of the Crock Pot.
3. Lay the roast on top of the vegetables.
4. In a small bowl, mix beef broth, Worcestershire sauce, thyme, and rosemary. Pour over the roast.
5. Cover and cook on low for 8 hours or until the meat is tender.
6. Serve the roast sliced with the vegetables on the side, drizzling with the juices from the pot.

Tender Pork Loin with Apples

For a delicious twist on pork, this recipe pairs tender pork loin with the natural sweetness of apples. The slow cooking process melds the flavors beautifully, creating a dish that's both savory and subtly sweet.

Ingredients:

- 2 lb pork loin
- 2 apples, sliced
- 1 large onion, sliced
- 1/2 cup apple cider or apple juice
- 1 tbsp Dijon mustard
- 1 tsp rosemary
- Salt and pepper to taste

Instructions:

1. Season the pork loin with salt, pepper, and rosemary.
2. Place the apple slices and onion at the bottom of the Crock Pot.
3. Lay the pork loin on top of the apples and onions.
4. Mix the apple cider and Dijon mustard, then pour over the pork.
5. Cover and cook on low for 6–8 hours or until the pork is tender.

6. Slice and serve, pairing each piece of pork with a bit of apple and onion.

Herb-Infused Lamb Roast

This herb-infused lamb roast is perfect for a special occasion or a comforting weekend dinner. The slow cooking process brings out the natural flavors of the lamb, complemented by fresh herbs and garlic.

Ingredients:

- 3 lb leg of lamb
- 4 garlic cloves, sliced
- 1 tbsp fresh rosemary, chopped
- 1 tbsp fresh thyme, chopped
- 1 cup chicken or beef broth
- Salt and pepper to taste

Instructions:

1. Cut small slits in the lamb and insert slices of garlic.
2. Season the lamb with salt, pepper, rosemary, and thyme.

3. Place the lamb in the Crock Pot and pour the broth around it.
4. Cover and cook on low for 7–8 hours until the lamb is tender and easily pulls apart.
5. Serve with juices from the pot, pairing well with roasted or mashed potatoes.

Simple BBQ Pulled Pork

BBQ pulled pork is a crowd-pleaser that's as versatile as it is delicious. This recipe yields juicy, flavorful pork that's perfect for sandwiches, tacos, or as a main dish with your favorite sides.

Ingredients:

- 3 lb pork shoulder (or pork butt)
- 1 cup BBQ sauce
- 1/2 cup apple cider vinegar
- 1/4 cup brown sugar
- 1 tsp smoked paprika
- 1/2 tsp garlic powder
- Salt and pepper to taste

> **Instructions:**

1. Rub the pork with salt, pepper, smoked paprika, and garlic powder.
2. Place the pork in the Crock Pot.
3. In a bowl, mix BBQ sauce, apple cider vinegar, and brown sugar, then pour over the pork.
4. Cover and cook on low for 8 hours until the pork is tender and falls apart easily.
5. Shred the pork with two forks and mix with the cooking juices for extra flavor.
6. Serve on buns with coleslaw, in tacos, or on its own.

Honey Garlic Chicken Thighs

Honey garlic chicken thighs are packed with flavor and require minimal prep. The honey adds a touch of sweetness, while garlic and soy sauce give the dish a savory kick.

Ingredients:

- 8 chicken thighs, bone-in, skin-on
- 1/2 cup honey
- 1/4 cup soy sauce
- 3 garlic cloves, minced
- 1 tsp ginger, minced
- Salt and pepper to taste
- Green onions and sesame seeds for garnish (optional)

Instructions:

1. Season the chicken thighs with salt and pepper.
2. Place them in the Crock Pot in a single layer, skin-side up.
3. In a small bowl, mix honey, soy sauce, garlic, and ginger. Pour over the chicken.
4. Cover and cook on low for 5–6 hours until the chicken is tender.
5. Garnish with green onions and sesame seeds before serving, if desired. Serve with rice or steamed vegetables.

Braised Short Ribs

Short ribs are ideal for slow cooking, becoming tender and flavorful as they braise. This dish is rich and hearty, perfect for a cold day.

Ingredients:

- 3 lb bone-in beef short ribs
- Salt and pepper to taste
- 1 large onion, chopped
- 3 carrots, chopped
- 2 celery stalks, chopped
- 3 garlic cloves, minced
- 1 cup beef broth
- 1/2 cup red wine (optional)
- 2 tbsp tomato paste
- 1 tsp thyme

Instructions:

1. Season the short ribs with salt and pepper.
2. Sear the short ribs in a skillet until browned, then transfer to the Crock Pot.
3. Add onion, carrots, celery, and garlic to the Crock Pot.

4. In a bowl, mix beef broth, red wine (if using), tomato paste, and thyme. Pour over the ribs and vegetables.
5. Cover and cook on low for 8–9 hours, until the meat is falling off the bone.
6. Serve the ribs with the vegetables and sauce from the pot.

Lemon Herb Turkey Breast

This lemon herb turkey breast is a lighter option that's flavorful and moist. It's an excellent choice for holiday dinners or a comforting weeknight meal.

Ingredients:
- 3 lb turkey breast, bone-in
- 1 lemon, sliced
- 2 tbsp olive oil
- 1 tsp rosemary
- 1 tsp thyme
- Salt and pepper to taste
- 1/2 cup chicken broth

Instructions:
1. Rub the turkey breast with olive oil, salt, pepper, rosemary, and thyme.
2. Place lemon slices in the bottom of the Crock Pot and lay the turkey breast on top.
3. Pour the chicken broth into the pot.
4. Cover and cook on low for 5–6 hours until the turkey is fully cooked and juicy.
5. Serve sliced with the lemony broth spooned over the top.

Italian Meatballs in Tomato Sauce

These Italian-style meatballs cook slowly in a rich tomato sauce, absorbing flavors for a melt-in-your-mouth texture. Serve them over pasta, on a sub, or enjoy them on their own.

Ingredients:
- 1 lb ground beef
- 1 lb ground pork
- 1/2 cup breadcrumbs
- 1/4 cup grated Parmesan cheese
- 2 eggs
- 3 garlic cloves, minced
- 1 tsp Italian seasoning

- Salt and pepper to taste
- 2 cups marinara sauce
- Fresh basil for garnish (optional)

Instructions:

1. In a bowl, mix ground beef, ground pork, breadcrumbs, Parmesan, eggs, garlic, Italian seasoning, salt, and pepper until well combined.
2. Form the mixture into 1.5-inch meatballs.
3. Place the meatballs in the Crock Pot and pour marinara sauce over them.
4. Cover and cook on low for 6–7 hours, until the meatballs are cooked through and tender.
5. Garnish with fresh basil and serve with pasta or crusty bread.

Each of these recipes is crafted to help you get the most flavor with minimal fuss. The Crock Pot brings out the natural flavors of each ingredient, making these meals a great addition to any dinner table. With these recipes in your rotation, you'll have everything you need to make satisfying meals with ease. Enjoy the process of slow cooking, knowing that each dish will be tender, flavorful, and comforting for everyone at the table.

CHAPTER FOUR: LIGHT AND FRESH DISHES

This chapter is all about flavorful, wholesome dishes that offer a lighter option for those days when you want something fresh and satisfying but not too heavy. Each recipe is designed to be easy on the palate and brings out the natural flavors of ingredients without overwhelming spices or sauces. Perfect for warm-weather days or when you're craving something bright and balanced, these recipes offer a variety of proteins and vegetables, giving you a range of options to enjoy.

Lemon Garlic Chicken Breast

This Lemon Garlic Chicken Breast is simple but packed with flavor. The zesty lemon and savory garlic pair beautifully to create a dish that's both refreshing and hearty.

Ingredients:
- 4 boneless, skinless chicken breasts
- 2 lemons (juice and zest)
- 4 cloves garlic, minced
- 2 tbsp olive oil
- 1 tsp dried thyme
- Salt and pepper to taste
- Fresh parsley for garnish

Instructions:
1. Place the chicken breasts in the Crock Pot.
2. In a small bowl, mix lemon juice, lemon zest, garlic, olive oil, thyme, salt, and pepper. Pour this mixture over the chicken.
3. Cover and cook on low for 4-5 hours or until chicken is tender.
4. Garnish with fresh parsley before serving.

Cooking Tip: For extra flavor, you can marinate the chicken in the lemon-garlic mixture for about 20 minutes before adding it to the Crock Pot. This simple preparation highlights the natural flavors, making it an ideal main course for any meal.

Vegetable Medley with Fresh Herbs

Perfect as a side or light main, this Vegetable Medley features an assortment of fresh vegetables, lightly seasoned with herbs. The slow cooking brings out their natural sweetness and makes each bite rich in flavor without adding extra calories.

Ingredients:
- 2 cups baby carrots
- 2 zucchinis, sliced
- 1 bell pepper, chopped
- 1 cup cherry tomatoes
- 1 red onion, sliced
- 1 tbsp olive oil
- 1 tsp dried oregano
- 1 tsp dried basil
- Salt and pepper to taste

Instructions:
1. Place all the vegetables in the Crock Pot.
2. Drizzle olive oil over the vegetables, then sprinkle oregano, basil, salt, and pepper. Toss lightly to coat.
3. Cover and cook on low for 3-4 hours, until vegetables are tender.
4. Serve as a side dish or enjoy as a light main course.

Cooking Tip: Experiment with any seasonal vegetables you have on hand. This dish is highly versatile, and each herb brings out the flavor of the vegetables without overpowering their natural taste.

Asian-Inspired Sweet and Sour Chicken

Bring a taste of Asia to your table with this Sweet and Sour Chicken. The sauce combines sweetness and tang with a bit of warmth from ginger, creating a balanced dish that pairs well with rice or steamed vegetables.

Ingredients:
- 4 chicken thighs, boneless and skinless
- 1 red bell pepper, chopped
- 1 green bell pepper, chopped
- 1/2 cup pineapple chunks
- 1/4 cup apple cider vinegar
- 3 tbsp honey
- 2 tbsp soy sauce
- 1 tbsp ketchup
- 1 tsp ginger, grated
- Salt and pepper to taste

Instructions:
1. Place the chicken, bell peppers, and pineapple chunks in the Crock Pot.
2. In a small bowl, whisk together apple cider vinegar, honey, soy sauce, ketchup, ginger, salt, and pepper. Pour over the chicken and vegetables.
3. Cover and cook on low for 4-5 hours, until the chicken is tender.
4. Serve with steamed rice or your favorite grain.

Cooking Tip: You can substitute the chicken with tofu or shrimp for a different protein option. Adjust the cooking time accordingly to prevent overcooking.

Mediterranean Ratatouille

Inspired by Mediterranean flavors, this Ratatouille is a nourishing dish full of vegetables like eggplant, zucchini, and bell peppers, simmered in a tomato base. The result is a richly flavored and healthful dish that can be enjoyed on its own or with a side of crusty bread.

Ingredients:

- 1 eggplant, diced
- 1 zucchini, sliced
- 1 red bell pepper, chopped
- 1 yellow bell pepper, chopped
- 1 onion, diced
- 1 can (14.5 oz) diced tomatoes
- 2 cloves garlic, minced
- 1 tsp dried thyme
- 1 tsp dried basil
- Salt and pepper to taste

Instructions:

1. Place the eggplant, zucchini, bell peppers, and onion in the Crock Pot.
2. Add the diced tomatoes, garlic, thyme, basil, salt, and pepper. Stir to combine.
3. Cover and cook on low for 5-6 hours, until the vegetables are soft and flavors are blended.
4. Serve as a main dish or as a side.

Cooking Tip: For extra depth, add a drizzle of olive oil before serving and sprinkle with fresh basil. This Ratatouille also pairs well with quinoa or couscous.

Stuffed Bell Peppers

These colorful Stuffed Bell Peppers are filled with a hearty blend of rice, vegetables, and spices. They make a satisfying, light main dish that's easy to prepare and cook.

Ingredients:
- 4 large bell peppers (any color), tops cut off and seeds removed
- 1 cup cooked rice
- 1/2 cup corn kernels
- 1/2 cup black beans, drained and rinsed
- 1/4 cup diced tomatoes
- 1/2 cup shredded cheese (optional)
- 1 tsp cumin
- 1/2 tsp chili powder
- Salt and pepper to taste

Instructions:
1. In a bowl, mix cooked rice, corn, black beans, diced tomatoes, cheese, cumin, chili powder, salt, and pepper.
2. Stuff each bell pepper with the rice mixture and place them upright in the Crock Pot.
3. Cover and cook on low for 4-5 hours, until the peppers are tender.

4. Garnish with fresh cilantro or green onions if desired.

Cooking Tip: You can vary the stuffing by adding ground turkey, cooked lentils, or even chopped mushrooms for more texture and flavor.

Zucchini Lasagna

A lighter twist on traditional lasagna, this Zucchini Lasagna replaces pasta with thin slices of zucchini, layering it with a tomato sauce and cheese for a satisfying, low-carb meal.

Ingredients:
- 3 medium zucchinis, thinly sliced lengthwise
- 1 cup ricotta cheese
- 1 cup shredded mozzarella cheese
- 1 egg
- 2 cups marinara sauce
- 1/2 tsp dried basil
- 1/2 tsp dried oregano
- Salt and pepper to taste

Instructions:
1. In a bowl, combine ricotta cheese, mozzarella, egg, basil, oregano, salt, and pepper.
2. Spread a thin layer of marinara sauce in the Crock Pot.
3. Layer zucchini slices, followed by a layer of the cheese mixture. Repeat until all ingredients are used, finishing with a layer of marinara sauce on top.
4. Cover and cook on low for 4-5 hours, until zucchini is tender.
5. Let cool slightly before serving.

Cooking Tip: For a heartier version, add cooked ground turkey or beef between layers. Serve with a side salad for a complete meal.

Lemon Dill Salmon

This Lemon Dill Salmon is an elegant yet simple dish, with tender, flaky salmon infused with the fresh flavors of lemon and dill. It's ideal for a light, nutritious meal.

Ingredients:
- 4 salmon fillets
- 2 lemons (sliced)
- 2 tbsp fresh dill, chopped
- 1 tbsp olive oil
- Salt and pepper to taste

Instructions:
1. Place lemon slices on the bottom of the Crock Pot, then lay the salmon fillets on top.
2. Drizzle with olive oil and season with salt, pepper, and fresh dill.
3. Cover and cook on low for 2-3 hours, or until salmon flakes easily with a fork.
4. Serve with a side of steamed vegetables or a fresh salad.

Cooking Tip: Salmon cooks quickly, so monitor it closely to avoid overcooking. This dish pairs well with quinoa or a simple couscous salad.

Quinoa and Black Bean Casserole

This Quinoa and Black Bean Casserole is a hearty, plant-based dish that's rich in protein and fiber. It's an excellent option for a light main course that's both filling and nutritious.

Ingredients:
- 1 cup quinoa, rinsed
- 1 can (15 oz) black beans, drained and rinsed
- 1 can (14.5 oz) diced tomatoes
- 1 cup corn kernels
- 1 red bell pepper, diced
- 1 tsp cumin
- 1/2 tsp paprika
- Salt and pepper to taste
- Fresh cilantro for garnish

Instructions:
1. Add quinoa, black beans, diced tomatoes, corn, bell pepper, cumin, paprika, salt, and pepper to the Crock Pot. Stir to combine.
2. Cover and cook on low for 4-5 hours, or until quinoa is tender.
3. Garnish with fresh cilantro before serving.

Cooking Tip: This casserole is versatile. Top with avocado or a dollop of Greek yogurt for added creaminess. It also works well as a filling for tacos or wraps.

CHAPTER FIVE: SIDES & VEGETABLES

Garlic Mashed Potatoes

Prep Time: 15 minutes
Cook Time: 3 hours (on high) or 5–6 hours (on low)
Servings: 6

Ingredients:
- 2 pounds russet potatoes, peeled and cubed
- 4 cloves garlic, minced
- 1 cup chicken or vegetable broth
- 1/2 cup whole milk
- 1/4 cup sour cream
- 4 tablespoons unsalted butter
- Salt and pepper, to taste
- Fresh chives or parsley, chopped, for garnish

Instructions:
1. Place the cubed potatoes and minced garlic in the Crock Pot. Pour in the broth, cover, and cook on high for 3 hours or low for 5–6 hours, until potatoes are tender.

2. Drain excess liquid, if any. Mash the potatoes directly in the Crock Pot using a masher or immersion blender.
3. Add milk, sour cream, and butter. Stir until smooth and creamy. Season with salt and pepper.
4. Garnish with fresh chives or parsley before serving. Enjoy warm as a perfect side for any main dish.

Tip: For extra creaminess, consider adding an extra tablespoon of butter or a splash of cream. Adjust seasoning to taste.

Creamed Spinach

Prep Time: 10 minutes
Cook Time: 2–3 hours (on high)
Servings: 4

Ingredients:
- 1-pound fresh spinach, roughly chopped
- 1 cup heavy cream
- 1/2 cup grated Parmesan cheese
- 1/4 cup cream cheese
- 3 cloves garlic, minced
- 1/4 teaspoon nutmeg

- Salt and pepper, to taste

Instructions:
1. Add the chopped spinach, heavy cream, Parmesan cheese, cream cheese, and minced garlic to the Crock Pot.
2. Sprinkle nutmeg, salt, and pepper over the top. Stir to combine.
3. Cover and cook on high for 2–3 hours, stirring occasionally, until the spinach is wilted and creamy.
4. Taste and adjust seasoning as needed. Serve warm as a comforting and delicious side.

Tip: If you prefer a thicker texture, stir in a bit more cream cheese or let the mixture cook uncovered for the last 15–20 minutes.

Green Bean Casserole

Prep Time: 15 minutes
Cook Time: 3–4 hours (on low)
Servings: 6

Ingredients:
- 1-pound fresh green beans, trimmed
- 1 can (10.5 ounces) cream of mushroom soup
- 1/2 cup milk
- 1/2 cup shredded cheddar cheese
- 1/2 cup crispy fried onions (plus extra for topping)
- Salt and pepper, to taste

Instructions:
1. Combine green beans, cream of mushroom soup, milk, shredded cheddar, and crispy fried onions in the Crock Pot.
2. Season with salt and pepper, then stir until everything is well mixed.
3. Cover and cook on low for 3–4 hours, until the green beans are tender and the sauce is creamy.
4. Before serving, sprinkle extra crispy fried onions on top for added texture.

Tip: For a richer casserole, add an extra handful of shredded cheddar or a few tablespoons of sour cream.

Herb Buttered Carrots

Prep Time: 10 minutes
Cook Time: 4 hours (on low)
Servings: 4

Ingredients:
- 1 pound baby carrots
- 3 tablespoons unsalted butter, melted
- 1 tablespoon honey
- 1 teaspoon dried thyme
- 1 teaspoon dried rosemary
- Salt and pepper, to taste

Instructions:
1. Place the baby carrots in the Crock Pot. Drizzle with melted butter and honey, then sprinkle with thyme, rosemary, salt, and pepper.
2. Stir to coat the carrots evenly with the butter and herbs.
3. Cover and cook on low for 4 hours, until carrots are tender.
4. Stir gently before serving to redistribute the buttery glaze.

Tip: Add a squeeze of lemon juice just before serving for a bit of brightness that complements the sweetness of the carrots.

Cheesy Cauliflower Bake

Prep Time: 15 minutes
Cook Time: 3 hours (on high) or 5–6 hours (on low)
Servings: 6

Ingredients:
- 1 head cauliflower, cut into florets
- 1 cup shredded sharp cheddar cheese
- 1/2 cup grated Parmesan cheese
- 1 cup heavy cream
- 3 cloves garlic, minced
- Salt and pepper, to taste
- Fresh parsley, chopped, for garnish

Instructions:
1. Place the cauliflower florets in the Crock Pot. Add the cheddar cheese, Parmesan cheese, heavy cream, and garlic.
2. Season with salt and pepper, then stir to combine everything.

3. Cover and cook on high for 3 hours or on low for 5–6 hours, until the cauliflower is tender and the cheese is melted and creamy.
4. Garnish with fresh parsley before serving.

Tip: For extra crunch, top with breadcrumbs or crushed crackers during the last 30 minutes of cooking.

Maple-Glazed Sweet Potatoes

Prep Time: 10 minutes
Cook Time: 4–5 hours (on low)
Servings: 4

Ingredients:
- 4 medium sweet potatoes, peeled and cubed
- 1/4 cup maple syrup
- 3 tablespoons unsalted butter, melted
- 1/2 teaspoon cinnamon
- Salt, to taste

Instructions:
1. Add the cubed sweet potatoes to the Crock Pot. Drizzle with maple syrup and melted butter, then sprinkle with cinnamon and a pinch of salt.

2. Stir to coat the sweet potatoes evenly.
3. Cover and cook on low for 4–5 hours, until the sweet potatoes are tender.
4. Serve warm, drizzling any leftover glaze from the pot over the top.

Tip: Add a sprinkle of chopped pecans during the last 30 minutes for a nutty crunch.

Brown Rice Pilaf with Veggies

Prep Time: 10 minutes
Cook Time: 3–4 hours (on high)
Servings: 6

Ingredients:
- 1 cup brown rice, rinsed
- 2 cups vegetable or chicken broth
- 1/2 cup diced onion
- 1/2 cup diced carrots
- 1/2 cup diced bell pepper
- 1 teaspoon dried basil
- 1/2 teaspoon dried thyme
- Salt and pepper, to taste

Instructions:
1. Combine the rinsed brown rice, broth, onion, carrots, bell pepper, basil, and thyme in the Crock Pot.
2. Season with salt and pepper, then stir to combine.
3. Cover and cook on high for 3–4 hours, until the rice is tender and the vegetables are cooked.
4. Fluff with a fork before serving.

Tip: Stir in a handful of fresh spinach or frozen peas just before serving for added color and nutrition.

Roasted Brussels Sprouts with Bacon

Prep Time: 10 minutes
Cook Time: 3–4 hours (on high)
Servings: 4

Ingredients:
- 1 pound Brussels sprouts, trimmed and halved
- 4 slices bacon, chopped
- 2 tablespoons olive oil
- Salt and pepper, to taste
- 1 tablespoon balsamic vinegar (optional)

Instructions:
1. Place the Brussels sprouts and chopped bacon in the Crock Pot. Drizzle with olive oil and season with salt and pepper.
2. Stir to coat the Brussels sprouts evenly.
3. Cover and cook on high for 3–4 hours, until the Brussels sprouts are tender and the bacon is crispy.
4. If desired, drizzle with balsamic vinegar before serving.

Tip: For extra caramelization, uncover the Crock Pot during the last 15–20 minutes of cooking to let excess moisture evaporate.

Each recipe in this chapter brings out the best of fresh ingredients with minimal fuss, allowing you to create comforting side dishes to complement any main course. From the creamy goodness of mashed potatoes to the nutty sweetness of maple-glazed sweet potatoes, these sides are a delightful addition to your table. Enjoy the ease of slow cooking, knowing that each dish is crafted with simplicity and flavor in mind.

CHAPTER SIX: SWEET TREATS & DESSERTS

In this chapter, you'll find delightful dessert recipes specially crafted for your Crock Pot. Each dessert combines the comfort of homemade sweets with the convenience of slow cooking, making it easier than ever to enjoy warm, delicious treats at the end of a meal or for special occasions. From fruit-filled cobblers to rich puddings, these recipes are designed to deliver satisfying flavors with minimal effort.

Apple Cinnamon Crisp

A classic dessert, apple cinnamon crisp brings together tender apples, a crunchy topping, and the warmth of cinnamon. With a Crock Pot, you'll get perfectly soft apples under a golden topping without the need to heat up your oven.

Ingredients:

- 6 medium apples, peeled and sliced
- 1/2 cup granulated sugar
- 1 tsp ground cinnamon
- 1/4 tsp nutmeg
- 1 cup rolled oats
- 1/2 cup all-purpose flour
- 1/2 cup brown sugar
- 1/4 cup butter, melted

Instructions:

1. Add the sliced apples, granulated sugar, cinnamon, and nutmeg to the Crock Pot. Stir to coat the apples evenly.
2. In a bowl, combine oats, flour, brown sugar, and melted butter until crumbly. Sprinkle the mixture over the apples.
3. Cover and cook on low for 3 hours, or until the apples are tender and the topping is golden and crisp.
4. Serve warm, optionally with a scoop of vanilla ice cream.

The slow-cooked apples blend beautifully with cinnamon, and the topping stays perfectly crisp, making this dessert a cozy treat.

Vanilla Rice Pudding

Vanilla rice pudding is a creamy, comforting dessert that's easy to prepare and rich in flavor. Cooking it slowly in a Crock Pot ensures that the rice becomes tender and the flavors meld together without constant stirring.

Ingredients:
- 1 cup Arborio rice (or other short-grain rice)
- 4 cups whole milk
- 1/2 cup granulated sugar
- 1 tsp vanilla extract
- 1/2 tsp ground cinnamon
- 1/4 tsp salt
- Optional toppings: raisins, fresh berries, or whipped cream

Instructions:
1. Add rice, milk, sugar, vanilla, cinnamon, and salt to the Crock Pot. Stir to combine.
2. Cover and cook on low for 3–4 hours, stirring once midway through cooking.
3. Once the pudding has thickened and the rice is tender, turn off the Crock Pot and allow the pudding to cool slightly.
4. Serve warm, with optional toppings like raisins or fresh berries.

The result is a rich and creamy rice pudding, flavored with vanilla and cinnamon, perfect for an after-dinner treat.

Chocolate Lava Cake

Chocolate lava cake is known for its gooey, molten center. Using the Crock Pot, you'll get a rich and indulgent dessert without the worry of overcooking.

Ingredients:
- 1 cup all-purpose flour
- 1/2 cup granulated sugar
- 1/4 cup cocoa powder
- 2 tsp baking powder

- 1/4 tsp salt
- 1/2 cup milk
- 1/4 cup melted butter
- 1 tsp vanilla extract
- 1/2 cup chocolate chips
- 1 cup boiling water

Instructions:

1. In a bowl, combine flour, sugar, cocoa powder, baking powder, and salt. Stir in milk, melted butter, and vanilla until smooth.
2. Pour the batter into the Crock Pot. Sprinkle chocolate chips over the batter.
3. Carefully pour boiling water over the batter, but do not stir.
4. Cover and cook on high for 2–3 hours, or until the edges are set and the center is still gooey.
5. Serve warm, scooping out portions to reveal the molten chocolate center.

This chocolate lava cake is sure to please anyone craving a decadent, chocolatey dessert.

Berry Cobbler

A cobbler is a perfect way to enjoy fresh or frozen berries, and the slow cooker method ensures that the fruit juices meld with the doughy topping for a warm and fruity dessert.

Ingredients:
- 4 cups mixed berries (strawberries, blueberries, blackberries, raspberries)
- 1/2 cup granulated sugar
- 1 tbsp lemon juice
- 1 cup all-purpose flour
- 1/4 cup granulated sugar (for the topping)
- 1 tsp baking powder
- 1/4 tsp salt
- 1/2 cup milk
- 1/4 cup melted butter

Instructions:
1. In the Crock Pot, combine berries, sugar, and lemon juice. Stir to coat the berries.
2. In a separate bowl, mix flour, sugar, baking powder, and salt. Stir in milk and melted butter until combined.
3. Drop spoonfuls of the batter over the berry mixture.

4. Cover and cook on low for 4 hours or until the topping is golden and cooked through.
5. Serve warm, optionally with whipped cream or vanilla ice cream.

This cobbler is a wonderful blend of tart berries and a lightly sweet topping—a crowd-pleaser for any occasion.

Pumpkin Spice Bread Pudding

Bread pudding is an ideal comfort dessert, and adding pumpkin spice brings a seasonal twist to this Crock Pot version. Soft bread cubes soak up a custard mixture, turning into a deliciously spiced, warm dessert.

Ingredients:
- 8 cups cubed day-old bread (French or brioche works well)
- 1 cup canned pumpkin puree
- 1 1/2 cups whole milk
- 1/2 cup heavy cream
- 1/2 cup brown sugar
- 1/4 cup granulated sugar
- 1 tsp vanilla extract

- 1 tsp pumpkin pie spice
- 1/4 tsp salt
- Optional topping: whipped cream or caramel sauce

Instructions:
1. In a large bowl, whisk together pumpkin puree, milk, heavy cream, brown sugar, granulated sugar, vanilla, pumpkin pie spice, and salt until smooth.
2. Add the bread cubes to the Crock Pot, then pour the custard mixture over the bread. Press gently to ensure all the bread is soaked.
3. Cover and cook on low for 3–4 hours, or until the bread pudding is set and slightly golden on top.
4. Serve warm, topped with whipped cream or a drizzle of caramel sauce.

This pumpkin spice bread pudding is a warm, flavorful dessert that's perfect for chilly evenings.

Caramelized Pears

Caramelized pears are a simple yet elegant dessert. Slow cooking the pears allows them to soften and absorb a rich caramel flavor, creating a treat that pairs beautifully with ice cream or yogurt.

Ingredients:
- 4 ripe pears, peeled and halved
- 1/2 cup brown sugar
- 1/4 cup unsalted butter, melted
- 1/2 tsp cinnamon
- 1/4 tsp nutmeg
- 1 tsp vanilla extract

Instructions:
1. Arrange pear halves in the Crock Pot in a single layer.
2. In a bowl, mix brown sugar, melted butter, cinnamon, nutmeg, and vanilla. Pour this mixture over the pears.
3. Cover and cook on low for 3 hours, or until pears are tender and caramelized.
4. Serve warm with a scoop of vanilla ice cream or a dollop of yogurt.

The slow cooking process brings out the natural sweetness of the pears, complemented by the caramel sauce for a simple yet refined dessert.

Banana Bread

Banana bread is a classic treat, and it's easily adapted to the Crock Pot. Cooking it slowly makes the loaf tender and moist, perfect for enjoying with a cup of tea or coffee.

Ingredients:
- 2 ripe bananas, mashed
- 1/4 cup melted butter
- 1/2 cup granulated sugar
- 1 tsp vanilla extract
- 1 cup all-purpose flour
- 1 tsp baking powder
- 1/4 tsp salt

Instructions:
1. In a mixing bowl, combine mashed bananas, melted butter, sugar, and vanilla.
2. In a separate bowl, whisk together flour, baking powder, and salt.
3. Gently fold the dry ingredients into the banana mixture until just combined.
4. Pour the batter into a greased loaf pan that fits into your Crock Pot. Place the pan in the Crock Pot and cover with the lid.

5. Cook on low for 3–4 hours, or until a toothpick inserted into the center comes out clean.
6. Let the banana bread cool slightly before slicing and serving.

This moist and flavorful banana bread is a delightful treat, perfect for a snack or light dessert.

Classic Bread Pudding

Classic bread pudding is an ultimate comfort dessert, turning stale bread into a custardy, rich treat. The Crock Pot allows the bread to soak up flavors, making it soft and delicious with every bite.

Ingredients:
- 8 cups cubed day-old bread
- 3 cups whole milk
- 3/4 cup granulated sugar
- 1/4 cup melted butter
- 3 large eggs
- 1 tsp vanilla extract
- 1/2 tsp cinnamon
- 1/4 tsp nutmeg
- Optional: raisins or chocolate chips

Instructions:
1. In a large bowl, whisk together milk, sugar, melted butter, eggs, vanilla, cinnamon, and nutmeg until smooth.
2. Add the cubed bread to the Crock Pot, and pour the custard mixture over it. Stir gently to ensure the bread is well-coated.
3. Cover and cook on low for 3–4 hours, or until the

CHAPTER SEVEN: HEALTHY OPTIONS FOR SPECIAL DIETS

As people's dietary needs change with age, adapting recipes to support wellness becomes essential. This chapter focuses on wholesome, Crock Pot-friendly recipes tailored to specific dietary requirements, including low-sodium, heart-healthy, gluten-free, low-carb, dairy-free, and high-fiber options. Each recipe is crafted with nutrient-dense ingredients that support wellness while delivering delicious flavors. Let's explore these meal options in detail.

Low-Sodium Beef Stew

Reducing sodium doesn't mean sacrificing flavor. This Low-Sodium Beef Stew uses fresh herbs, garlic, and vegetables to build a robust, savory taste that doesn't rely on salt.

Ingredients:
- 1 lb lean beef stew meat, trimmed and cut into 1-inch cubes
- 2 large carrots, sliced
- 2 potatoes, diced

- 1 onion, chopped
- 2 celery stalks, chopped
- 3 cloves garlic, minced
- 2 cups low-sodium beef broth
- 1 cup water
- 1 tsp thyme
- 1 tsp rosemary
- Black pepper to taste

Instructions:
1. Place the beef, carrots, potatoes, onion, and celery in the Crock Pot.
2. Add minced garlic, thyme, rosemary, and black pepper.
3. Pour in the low-sodium beef broth and water, stirring to combine.
4. Cover and cook on low for 7-8 hours, until beef and vegetables are tender.

Tip: For more flavor, brown the beef in a skillet before adding it to the Crock Pot. This step caramelizes the meat's surface, adding a deeper taste without extra sodium.

Heart-Healthy Chicken and Vegetables

A meal loaded with lean proteins and vegetables, this Heart-Healthy Chicken and Vegetables recipe provides nutrients essential for cardiovascular wellness. By using olive oil and herbs, you can create a satisfying dish that's light on saturated fats.

Ingredients:
- 4 boneless, skinless chicken breasts
- 2 zucchini, sliced
- 1 red bell pepper, chopped
- 1 yellow bell pepper, chopped
- 1 cup cherry tomatoes
- 1 onion, sliced
- 3 cloves garlic, minced
- 2 tbsp olive oil
- 1 tsp basil
- 1 tsp oregano
- 1/2 tsp black pepper
- Juice of 1 lemon

Instructions:
1. Arrange the chicken breasts at the bottom of the Crock Pot.
2. Top with zucchini, bell peppers, cherry tomatoes, and onion.
3. Add garlic, basil, oregano, and black pepper.
4. Drizzle olive oil and lemon juice over the ingredients.
5. Cover and cook on low for 6 hours, until the chicken is cooked through and vegetables are tender.

Tip: Add a handful of spinach during the last 15 minutes of cooking for an extra boost of heart-healthy nutrients like iron and potassium.

Gluten-Free Chili

This hearty chili is perfect for those with gluten sensitivities. Made with beans, lean meat, and gluten-free spices, it offers a filling meal that's both rich in fiber and full of flavor.

Ingredients:
- 1 lb ground turkey or lean beef
- 1 bell pepper, chopped
- 1 onion, chopped
- 3 cloves garlic, minced
- 1 can (15 oz) kidney beans, rinsed and drained
- 1 can (15 oz) black beans, rinsed and drained
- 1 can (15 oz) diced tomatoes
- 1 cup gluten-free beef or vegetable broth
- 1 tbsp chili powder
- 1 tsp cumin
- 1/2 tsp smoked paprika
- Salt and black pepper to taste

Instructions:
1. If desired, brown the ground meat in a skillet and drain any excess fat.
2. Place the meat, bell pepper, onion, garlic, beans, diced tomatoes, and broth in the Crock Pot.
3. Add chili powder, cumin, smoked paprika, salt, and pepper.
4. Stir well, cover, and cook on low for 6-8 hours, until flavors meld.

Tip: To spice it up, add a chopped jalapeno or a pinch of cayenne pepper.

Low-Carb Chicken Alfredo

For those watching carbs, this creamy, low-carb Chicken Alfredo offers all the indulgence of traditional Alfredo sauce without the pasta. Serve it with spiralized zucchini or cauliflower rice for a satisfying meal.

Ingredients:
- 4 boneless, skinless chicken breasts
- 1 cup unsweetened almond milk
- 1/2 cup heavy cream or coconut cream (for dairy-free option)
- 3 cloves garlic, minced
- 1/4 cup grated Parmesan cheese (optional)
- 1 tsp Italian seasoning
- Salt and black pepper to taste
- Chopped parsley for garnish

Instructions:
1. Place the chicken breasts in the Crock Pot.
2. In a bowl, mix almond milk, heavy cream, garlic, Parmesan cheese, Italian seasoning, salt, and pepper.
3. Pour the sauce over the chicken.
4. Cover and cook on low for 5-6 hours, until chicken is tender.

5. Shred the chicken with two forks, stir well, and garnish with parsley.

Tip: Serve with spiralized zucchini or steamed cauliflower to keep the dish low-carb and satisfying.

Dairy-Free Vegetable Soup

This vegetable soup is creamy and comforting without any dairy. Perfect for those with lactose intolerance or a dairy-free diet, it relies on blended potatoes and vegetables to give it a thick, smooth texture.

Ingredients:
- 1 large potato, peeled and diced
- 1 zucchini, sliced
- 2 carrots, sliced
- 1 onion, chopped
- 2 cups chopped broccoli
- 3 cups vegetable broth
- 1 cup coconut milk
- Salt and black pepper to taste
- Fresh parsley for garnish

Instructions:
1. Place potato, zucchini, carrots, onion, and broccoli in the Crock Pot.
2. Pour vegetable broth over the vegetables.
3. Cover and cook on low for 6-7 hours, until vegetables are very tender.
4. Use an immersion blender to puree the soup to a smooth consistency.
5. Stir in coconut milk, add salt and pepper, and garnish with fresh parsley.

Tip: For a chunkier soup, blend half the mixture and leave the rest intact for more texture.

Mediterranean-Inspired Chickpea Stew

Chickpeas are rich in protein and fiber, making them a wonderful base for a vegetarian dish. This Mediterranean-inspired stew combines chickpeas with tomatoes, olives, and spices for a dish packed with flavor.

Ingredients:
- 2 cans (15 oz each) chickpeas, drained and rinsed
- 1 can (15 oz) diced tomatoes

- 1 bell pepper, chopped
- 1 onion, chopped
- 1/2 cup pitted black olives
- 3 cloves garlic, minced
- 1 tsp cumin
- 1 tsp smoked paprika
- 1/2 tsp turmeric
- 2 cups vegetable broth
- Fresh cilantro for garnish

Instructions:
1. Place chickpeas, tomatoes, bell pepper, onion, olives, and garlic in the Crock Pot.
2. Add cumin, smoked paprika, turmeric, and vegetable broth.
3. Stir to combine, cover, and cook on low for 6-7 hours.
4. Garnish with fresh cilantro before serving.

Tip: Serve over quinoa or couscous for a complete Mediterranean-inspired meal.

High-Protein Bean Soup

Beans are an excellent source of plant-based protein. This High-Protein Bean Soup combines multiple varieties of beans to create a hearty, nutritious dish that's filling and packed with flavor.

Ingredients:
- 1 can (15 oz) kidney beans, drained and rinsed
- 1 can (15 oz) white beans, drained and rinsed
- 1 can (15 oz) black beans, drained and rinsed
- 1 can (15 oz) diced tomatoes
- 1 onion, chopped
- 3 cloves garlic, minced
- 2 carrots, sliced
- 1 tsp thyme
- 1 tsp oregano
- 2 cups vegetable broth
- Salt and black pepper to taste

Instructions:
1. Combine kidney beans, white beans, black beans, diced tomatoes, onion, garlic, and carrots in the Crock Pot.
2. Add thyme, oregano, vegetable broth, salt, and pepper.

3. Stir well, cover, and cook on low for 7-8 hours, until flavors meld and soup thickens.

Tip: Add a handful of chopped kale or spinach during the last 30 minutes for added nutrients.

Fiber-Rich Lentil Soup

Lentils are high in fiber and perfect for creating a hearty, satisfying soup. This Fiber-Rich Lentil Soup includes a blend of vegetables and spices to make a nutritious, filling dish.

Ingredients:
- 1 cup dried lentils, rinsed
- 1 onion, chopped
- 2 carrots, sliced
- 2 celery stalks, chopped
- 3 cloves garlic, minced
- 1 can (15 oz) diced tomatoes
- 1 tsp cumin
- 1/2 tsp turmeric
- 1/2 tsp paprika
- 4 cups vegetable broth
- Fresh parsley for garnish

Instructions:

1. Place lentils, onion, carrots, celery, garlic, and diced tomatoes in the Crock Pot.

2. Add cumin, turmeric, paprika, and vegetable broth.

3. Stir to combine, cover, and cook on low for 6-8 hours, until lentils are tender.

4.

CHAPTER EIGHT: TIME-SAVING TIPS AND MEAL PREP

In this chapter, you'll find practical advice to make the most of your Crock Pot, whether you're preparing meals ahead of time, cooking in batches, or looking for tips to enhance flavors. With the right strategies, you can streamline your cooking routine, cut down on prep time, and ensure every dish is packed with flavor. From freezer-friendly recipes to storage hacks, these insights will help you feel confident and efficient in the kitchen.

Make-Ahead Meals for Busy Days

Meal prepping with a Crock Pot is ideal for those days when you know you'll be pressed for time but still want a home-cooked meal waiting for you. By dedicating a little time upfront to prepare ingredients or even fully cooked dishes, you'll free yourself from daily prep. Here's how you can make your Crock Pot work for you in advance:

1. Prepare Ingredients the Night Before
   - Chop vegetables, trim and season meat, and measure out spices or sauces the night before. Store everything in sealed containers in the fridge so that all you need to do is dump the ingredients into the Crock Pot in the morning.

2. Assemble and Refrigerate Meals in Labeled Bags
   - For an even faster morning, place all ingredients for a recipe into a resealable freezer or storage bag. Label the bag with the recipe name, cooking instructions, and date, then refrigerate overnight. In the morning, pour the contents into the Crock Pot and set it on low. This method also works well with freezer meals, which we'll cover in the next section.

3. Pre-Cook Certain Ingredients
   - While the Crock Pot handles raw ingredients well, some dishes benefit from a little pre-cooking. For instance, browning meat or onions can add depth to a recipe. Do this step the night before to avoid having to take extra steps in the morning.

4. Plan for Leftovers
   - Some dishes, like chili, soups, and stews, actually taste better the next day as flavors meld. Plan to cook enough for multiple meals, so you have

leftovers that can easily be reheated for lunch or dinner.

5. Label with Cooking Times
 - If you're making multiple meals ahead of time, label each container with cooking times. This small step helps you keep track of which meals require shorter or longer cook times, especially if you have meals that require only a few hours.

Freezer-Friendly Crock Pot Recipes

Freezer meals are one of the best ways to save time, allowing you to prep in bulk and have meals ready at a moment's notice. These meals can be made entirely in advance and frozen until needed. Here's how to set up your freezer for slow-cooking success:

1. Select Freezer-Friendly Ingredients
 - Some ingredients freeze better than others. Vegetables like carrots, celery, and bell peppers retain their texture well, while zucchini and leafy greens can become mushy. Meats, soups, and stews generally freeze well and taste great when reheated.

2. Assemble and Freeze Raw Ingredients
 - Many freezer meals involve placing all raw ingredients in a freezer bag, which saves time later. For example, you can assemble a beef stew by adding diced beef, carrots, onions, potatoes, and broth in a freezer bag. Then, label and freeze it. On cooking day, simply add the contents to your Crock Pot.

3. Use Freezer Bags to Save Space
 - To maximize freezer space, use gallon-sized freezer bags and freeze meals flat. Once frozen, they can be stacked or stored upright like books, saving space in your freezer.

4. Label Bags with Cooking Instructions
 - Always label bags with the recipe name, date, and cooking instructions. Include whether it should be cooked on high or low and any additional steps, like adding fresh herbs at the end. This way, there's no guesswork involved when you're ready to cook.

5. Thaw Before Cooking
 - Thawing meals overnight in the fridge helps them cook evenly in the Crock Pot. Freezing can make some ingredients cook unevenly if they're placed directly in the Crock Pot, especially when cooking on low.

6. Create a Freezer Meal Rotation
   - To keep things interesting, rotate your freezer meals regularly, using them within a few weeks of freezing for the best texture and flavor. Having a variety of meals on hand will ensure you always have something delicious ready to go.

Batch Cooking Tips

Batch cooking is a great way to ensure you have ready-to-eat meals or base ingredients that can be used in multiple recipes throughout the week. Using your Crock Pot to batch-cook meals saves you both time and effort. Here's how to get the most out of this method:

1. Cook Multiple Recipes at Once
   - If you have more than one Crock Pot, use them simultaneously to prepare different recipes. For instance, cook a soup in one Crock Pot and a roast in another. This way, you'll have a variety of meals to eat or freeze.

2. Prepare Staple Ingredients
   - Cooking a large batch of staple ingredients, like shredded chicken, beans, or rice, allows you to create multiple meals throughout the week. Shredded chicken can be used in salads, tacos, or casseroles, while cooked beans work well in soups and stews.

3. Portion and Freeze
   - Divide batch-cooked meals into individual or family-sized portions, and freeze them. Portioning makes it easier to thaw only what you need, reducing waste and ensuring you have ready-to-eat meals.

4. Label Each Batch with Date and Recipe
   - Proper labeling helps you keep track of what's in the freezer and when it was prepared. Use freezer-safe containers or bags, and include cooking instructions or reheating times for added convenience.

5. Rotate Your Freezer Stock
   - When batch-cooking, it's easy to forget meals at the back of the freezer. Place newer meals toward the back, moving older ones to the front. This rotation ensures that meals are used before they lose quality.

Maximizing Flavor in Your Dishes

Although Crock Pots cook slowly, they don't always amplify flavors the way other cooking methods might. Here are ways to bring out the best flavors in your dishes:

1. Brown Meat Before Slow Cooking
   - While it's tempting to skip browning, taking this extra step caramelizes the surface of the meat, adding depth and a richer flavor. This step is especially important for beef and pork roasts.

2. Use Fresh Herbs at the End
   - Adding herbs like parsley, basil, or cilantro at the end of cooking preserves their fresh flavor, which can be lost during long cooking times. Just a handful of fresh herbs can brighten up the entire dish.

3. Experiment with Acids
   - A small amount of vinegar, lemon juice, or lime juice added toward the end of cooking can add balance and enhance other flavors. Acids are especially useful in meat dishes and stews.

4. Adjust Seasoning
 - Salt and pepper should be adjusted before serving, as flavors can mellow during long cooking. Tasting and seasoning at the end allows you to achieve the perfect balance.

5. Layer Flavors with Aromatics
 - Layering ingredients like onions, garlic, and ginger provides a base flavor that develops over time. Add these at the beginning of cooking to allow the flavors to meld into the dish.

6. Finish with a Splash of Cream or Coconut Milk
 - Creamy ingredients add body and smoothness to soups and curries. Stirring in a little coconut milk, heavy cream, or even Greek yogurt at the end can enrich the texture and flavor.

Tips for Cooking Different Types of Meat

Different meats require different approaches when using a Crock Pot. Here's how to handle various types for the best results:

1. Chicken
   - Boneless chicken breasts cook quickly, usually needing only 3–4 hours on low. For more flavor, use bone-in, skin-on chicken pieces and cook them for 6–8 hours. Chicken thighs are also a great option for long cooking times, as they retain moisture better than breast meat.

2. Beef
   - Cuts like chuck roast, short ribs, and brisket are ideal for slow cooking. These tougher cuts become tender and flavorful over 8–10 hours on low. Avoid using tender cuts like sirloin, as they may become tough and dry.

3. Pork
   - Pork shoulder and pork butt are excellent for slow-cooking, especially in recipes like pulled pork. These cuts have enough fat to stay moist and flavorful, even with long cooking times. Pork chops, on the other hand, can become dry and are better suited to shorter cooking times.

4. Lamb
   - Lamb shanks, shoulder, and neck are perfect for Crock Pot recipes. They become tender with long cooking, taking on the flavors of herbs and spices. Avoid using leaner cuts like loin, as they can dry out.

5. Seafood
   - Seafood generally cooks too quickly for the Crock Pot, but certain recipes work well with shrimp or white fish added in the last 30 minutes of cooking. Shellfish like clams and mussels should also be added late to prevent them from overcooking.

Cleanup and Storage Hacks

Cleaning up after a Crock Pot meal can be quick and easy with a few tricks:

1. Use Crock Pot Liners
   - Disposable liners are a convenient way to reduce cleanup time. They prevent food from sticking to the sides of the pot, making it easy to serve meals and wash up afterward.

2. Soak Immediately After Cooking
   - After transferring food, fill the Crock Pot with warm soapy water and let it soak. This helps loosen any stuck-on bits, making it easier to clean.

CHAPTER NINE: CONCLUSION

As we come to the end of this cookbook, it's time to reflect on the journey we've taken through the wonderful world of Crock Pot cooking. The goal of this book has been to empower you to harness the convenience and versatility of your Crock Pot, enabling you to create delicious, home-cooked meals with ease and confidence. Whether you're a seasoned cook or a beginner, the recipes and tips provided here are designed to simplify your cooking experience and enhance your enjoyment of food.

Throughout this journey, we've explored a variety of recipes tailored to suit different tastes, occasions, and dietary needs. From hearty soups and savory roasts to delectable desserts and healthy options, each dish offers an opportunity to nourish yourself and your loved ones. The beauty of the Crock Pot lies in its ability to bring flavors together over time, resulting in comforting meals that evoke warmth and satisfaction.

Embracing the Convenience of Slow Cooking

One of the most significant advantages of using a Crock Pot is the convenience it offers. With the busy lifestyles many of us lead, finding time to prepare wholesome meals can often feel overwhelming. The Crock Pot allows you to "set it and forget it," freeing up your time for other activities. Imagine coming home after a long day to the enticing aroma of a meal that's been cooking all day, ready to serve with minimal effort. This simplicity is especially beneficial for women over 70, who may appreciate the ease of preparing meals without extensive standing or hands-on cooking.

Encouragement to Explore and Experiment

While this cookbook provides a solid foundation of recipes and techniques, the true magic of cooking lies in your willingness to explore and experiment. Use the recipes as a guide, but don't hesitate to make them your own. Adjust flavors, try new ingredients, or combine elements from different recipes to suit your preferences. The more you experiment, the more comfortable you will become in the kitchen, and the more enjoyment you will find in the process of cooking.

Cooking is not only about preparing food; it's about creating memories, sharing experiences, and nurturing relationships. Invite family and friends to join you in the kitchen, turning meal prep into a social activity. Whether it's preparing a meal together or sharing a delicious dish, these moments can foster connections and create cherished memories.

Final Thoughts and Closing Remarks

As you embark on your culinary adventures with your Crock Pot, remember that every meal is an opportunity to nourish yourself and those around you. Embrace the joy of cooking, the satisfaction of preparing a meal from scratch, and the comfort of sharing food with loved ones. Your Crock Pot is not just a kitchen appliance; it's a tool that can help you explore new flavors, try new recipes, and enjoy the art of cooking without stress.

In closing, we hope this book has inspired you to make the most of your Crock Pot and to embrace the convenience and satisfaction it offers. As you prepare meals using the recipes and tips outlined in this cookbook, may you find joy in the process, delight in the flavors, and comfort in the home-cooked meals that bring people together. Happy cooking, and may your Crock Pot serve you well for many delicious meals to come!

REVIEW

What Readers Are Saying

A must-read! This book is packed with valuable insights and practical advice. It's clear, engaging, and easy to follow. Highly recommend!

Absolutely loved it! The content is well-organized and provides real solutions. Perfect for anyone looking to improve their life.

A game-changer! The author delivers thoughtful, relatable advice that makes a real impact. I've learned so much.

This book exceeded my expectations. It's clear, concise, and filled with actionable tips. A great resource for beginners and experts alike!

Incredibly helpful and inspiring. This book has become my go-to guide. Highly recommend to anyone seeking practical solutions and positive change.

Made in the USA
Columbia, SC
23 April 2025

002f37cd-3a45-421c-ac61-80574b123091R01